Out and About at the HOSPITAL

by Nancy Garhan Attebury

illustrated by Zachary Trover

Special thanks to our advisers for their expertise:

Laurie L. Bentdahl, L.P.N.
Mankato, Minnesota

Susan Kesselring, M.A., Literacy Educator
Rosemount–Apple Valley–Eagan (Minnesota) School District

PICTURE WINDOW BOOKS
Minneapolis, Minnesota

The author wishes to thank the Attebury family, the Garhan family, Dr. William Pettit, and Dr. Patrick McCarthy.

Editorial Director: Carol Jones
Managing Editor: Catherine Neitge
Creative Director: Keith Griffin
Editor: Jill Kalz
Story Consultant: Terry Flaherty
Designer: Zachary Trover
Page Production: Picture Window Books
The illustrations in this book were created digitally.

Picture Window Books
5115 Excelsior Boulevard
Suite 232
Minneapolis, MN 55416
877-845-8392
www.picturewindowbooks.com

Printed in the United States of America.

Library of Congress Cataloging-in-Publication Data
Attebury, Nancy Garhan.
Out and about at the hospital / by Nancy Garhan Attebury ; illustrated by Zachary Trover.
p. cm. — (Field trips)
ISBN 1-4048-1148-6 (hardcover)
1. Hospitals—Juvenile literature. 2. Hospital care—Juvenile literature. I. Trover, Zachary.
II. Title. III. Field trips (Picture Window Books)
RA963.5.G37 2006
362.11—dc22   2005004264

We're going on a field trip to the hospital. We can't wait!

Things to find out:

Why do people go to the hospital?

Who works at the hospital?

Where do people go if they have an emergency?

What happens if we have to stay at the hospital overnight?

Welcome to Brown Hospital! My name is Ari, and I'm a nurse. At Brown, we take care of people who need medical help or an operation. The people we help are called patients.

We also help people who have an injury. Have any of you ever been here to get stitches? Lots of kids have.

Stitches made of plastic or thread are used to sew up a cut so it heals better. Doctors and nurses call stitches "sutures." Stitches are taken out after 3 to 14 days. Some kinds of stitches slowly disappear as the cut heals.

5

The first thing I'll show you is the admissions desk. Before we can help you, you must be admitted, or checked in. Jolie is an admissions clerk. She'll ask for your name, your date of birth, and the name of your doctor. Then she'll ask why you are here.

ADMISSIONS

After that, Jolie snaps a plastic bracelet on your wrist. It shows your name and medical information. You wear it so doctors and nurses know who you are and how to help you. Jolie may also give you an allergy bracelet. It lists any allergies you may have.

Kids have their own special kind of doctor called a pediatrician. A pediatrician gives medical care to kids from birth through their teenage years.

7

But what if you're injured or very sick? What if you can't check yourself in? If that's the case, our emergency department is your first stop.

8

There's always someone here to help you in the emergency department. Ken is one of our nurses. He can put a brace or cast on broken bones. He can take vital signs. If the doctor says it's OK, he can even give medicine to patients. Ken is great at staying calm in an emergency.

Emergency departments can help with just about any medical emergency: cuts, broken bones, heart and breathing problems, gunshot wounds, animal bites, stomach trouble, and much more.

We keep hospital supplies in the supply room. It's quiet now, but it can get very busy. Shelves must be kept neat and orderly so nurses can find what they need quickly. See how everything is labeled?

Medicine used at the hospital is kept in special locked cabinets. Only certain hospital workers can open these cabinets, which makes it easier to keep track of where the medicine goes.

This is the operating room. We call it the OR for short. You can see that it's very clean and bright.

Doctors and nurses who work in the OR wear caps, masks, plastic gloves, special tops and pants, and shoe covers. Everything is sterile. We want the OR to be free of germs so patients who have an operation don't get an infection.

O.R. #1

Tools used during an operation must be sterile. They are put in a kind of large dishwasher. The machine uses steam or chemicals to sterilize them. Infections are rare when equipment and clothing are sterile.

13

If you have to stay overnight, you'll get a bed in our kids' section, called Pediatrics. Your mom or dad can stay with you. Parents, doctors, and nurses want kids to be safe and comfortable in the hospital. Some kids have their own room. Others share.

14

Jared and Mark are sharing this room. Jared had his tonsils taken out this morning. Mark had an operation yesterday to remove his appendix. His belly is still a little sore.

Patients who stay overnight at the hospital wear a hospital gown. The gown makes it easy for nurses and doctors to give patients shots or listen to their heart. It usually opens in the back.

Each patient has a medical chart. The chart lists the patient's name, the doctor's name, what kind of medicine the patient needs, how much, and when to give it.

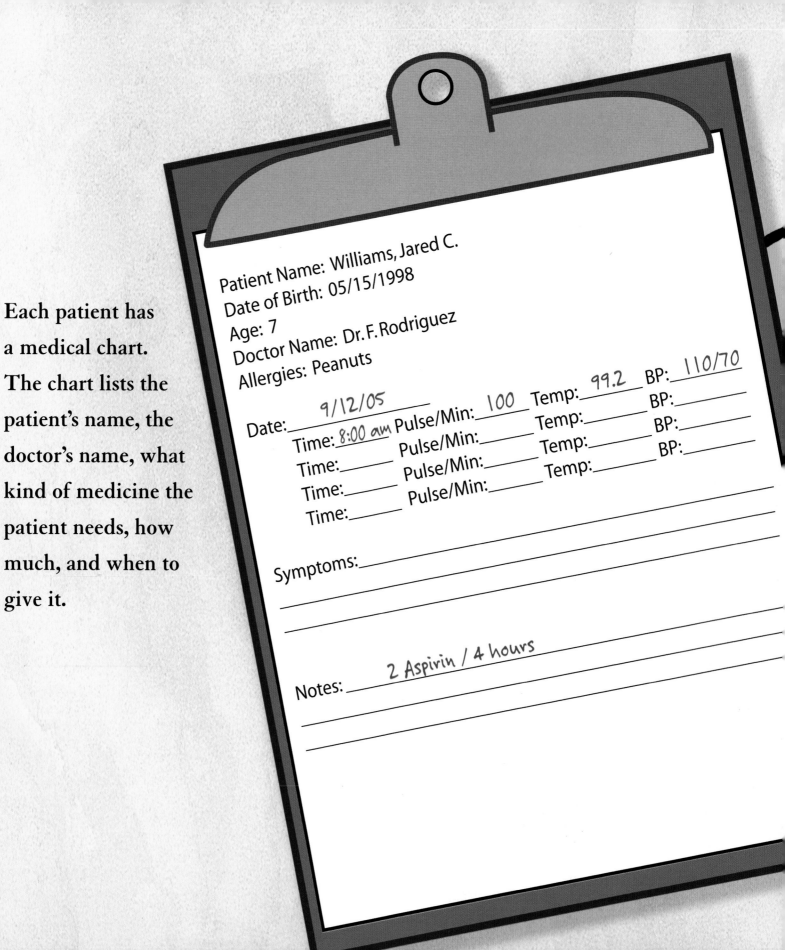

Patient Name: Williams, Jared C.
Date of Birth: 05/15/1998
Age: 7
Doctor Name: Dr. F. Rodriguez
Allergies: Peanuts

Date: _9/12/05_
Time: _8:00 am_ Pulse/Min: _100_ Temp: _99.2_ BP: _110/70_
Time: _____ Pulse/Min: _____ Temp: _____ BP: _____
Time: _____ Pulse/Min: _____ Temp: _____ BP: _____
Time: _____ Pulse/Min: _____ Temp: _____ BP: _____
Time: _____ Pulse/Min: _____

Symptoms: _____
_____
_____

Notes: _2 Aspirin / 4 hours_
_____
_____

Vital signs are written on the medical chart many times a day. There is also space to list a patient's allergies.

Nurses take vitals with a:

- **blood pressure cuff**
used to measure how well a patient's heart can pump blood
- **thermometer**
used to take a patient's temperature
- **watch with a second hand**
used to count a patient's pulse rate
- **stethoscope**
used to listen to a patient's heartbeat

Here comes Ben with lunch trays! Not all hospital patients get the same food. Jared gets a cherry Popsicle for lunch. The flavored ice will feel good sliding down his sore throat. Mark's lunch is toast, soup, and pudding.

18

When family and friends come to visit, they can buy sandwiches or snacks in the cafeteria. We also have a gift shop filled with flowers, cards, and stuffed animals.

Doctors decide what kind of medicine to give their patients. The dose, or amount of medicine, can depend on how much a patient weighs. For example, a child wouldn't need as much as a full-grown adult.

19

Doctors and nurses are a lot like detectives. They solve mysteries when they study vital signs and symptoms to learn what is wrong with a patient. They do tests. And they talk to the patient and ask how he or she feels.

The hospital is a big, busy place. But remember: we're here to help if you need us. Thanks for visiting today!

KEEPING YOUR OWN MEDICAL CHART

Nurses and doctors check a patient's vital signs many times a day. Pretend you are checking two vital signs of a patient—and the patient is you!

What you need:

a blank piece of paper
a pencil or pen
a ruler
a clock or watch with a second hand
a fever strip or regular thermometer

What you do:

1. Use the paper, pencil, and ruler to draw a chart like the one on page 16.
2. At 8:00 A.M. on Day 1, sit still for five minutes. Then, use your index finger and middle finger to check your pulse. You can feel the beat at your neck, wrist, or ankle. Ask an adult to help you find it. Use the watch to count your pulse for 15 seconds. Multiply that number by four to get the rate per minute. Write the results on your chart.
3. Have an adult help you take your temperature. Write the results on your chart.
4. Write any symptoms you may feel, such as "tired," "dizzy," or "OK."
5. At 12:00 noon, walk around in your house or neighborhood for five minutes. Then, take your pulse and temperature, and write the results on your chart. Write any symptoms you might have, too.
6. At 5:00 P.M., do 20 sit-ups or 20 jumping jacks. Take your pulse and temperature. Write the results, along with any symptoms.
7. At 8:00 P.M., sit quietly for five minutes, and then take your pulse and temperature. Write any symptoms.
8. Repeat this whole routine for three days in a row. Do you notice any change from day to day? Share your results with an adult. How does physical activity change a person's vital signs?

FUN FACTS

- A general hospital is one that handles many kinds of medical problems, accidents, diseases, and illnesses. Special hospitals handle one kind of medical condition. A pediatric hospital is one that only takes care of children.

- Patients in the hospital get a "condition rank" to describe how they are doing. Ranks include "critical" (very sick), "stable" (staying the same), "satisfactory" (less sick), "fair" (OK), and "good/excellent" (ready to go home).

- Hospitals are usually divided into sections called units or wings. The labor and delivery unit takes care of women and their babies before and during childbirth. Close to four million babies are born in U.S. hospitals each year.

- People who want to become doctors train for many years. They take four years of college classes and then four years of medical school classes. Depending on what kind of doctor they want to be, they still need three to eight more years of training before they become doctors.

GLOSSARY

admitted—signed in

allergies—having reactions such as a runny nose, watery eyes, or a rash when around, or when eating, certain things; people may be allergic to plants, animals, dust, or certain kinds of food

blood pressure—how hard the blood is pushing against the walls of the tiny tubes (veins and arteries) in which it flows throughout the body

medical chart—a paper form on which a patient's information is written

patient—a person who needs medical care

pulse—the steady beat of blood moving through the body

sterile—germfree

symptoms—signs that a person may have an illness; for example, a rash or fever

vital signs—a person's pulse rate, blood pressure, heart rate, and temperature; also called vitals

TO LEARN MORE

At the Library

Amos, Janine. *The Hospital*. Milwaukee, Wis.: Gareth Stevens Publishing, 2002.

Gibson, Karen Bush. *Emergency Medical Technicians*. Mankato, Minn.: Bridgestone Books, 2001.

Rosinsky, Natalie M. *A Hospital*. Mankato, Minn.: Smart Apple Media, 2003.

Watson, Kim. *A Trip to the Hospital*. New York: Simon Spotlight/Nick Jr., 2001.

On the Web

FactHound offers a safe, fun way to find Web sites related to this book. All of the sites on FactHound have been researched by our staff. *www.facthound.com*

1. Visit the FactHound home page.
2. Enter a search word related to this book, or type in this special code: 1404811486.
3. Click on the FETCH IT button.

Your trusty FactHound will fetch the best sites for you!

INDEX

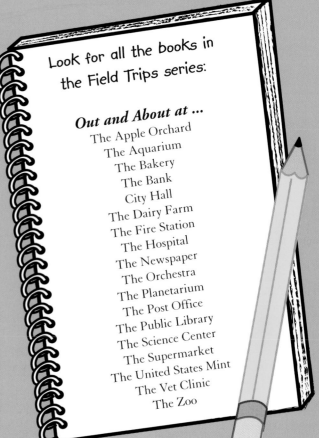

Look for all the books in the Field Trips series:

Out and About at ...
The Apple Orchard
The Aquarium
The Bakery
The Bank
City Hall
The Dairy Farm
The Fire Station
The Hospital
The Newspaper
The Orchestra
The Planetarium
The Post Office
The Public Library
The Science Center
The Supermarket
The United States Mint
The Vet Clinic
The Zoo